9297

AN INSTANT GUIDE TO

FRESHWATER BIRDS

The most common inland water
birds of North America
described and illustrated in full color

Mike Lambert and Alan Pearson

BONANZA BOOKS
New York

First published 1988 by Bonanza Books,
distributed by Crown Publishers, Inc.

Printed in Spain

ISBN 0–517–66792–4

h g f e d c b a

Contents

Introduction

Out for a walk by the pond in your local park or on vacation near a lake or a river, you will see many of the birds that live in and around water. Of course, everyone knows — or thinks they know — what a duck looks like; but do you know the difference between, say, a Mallard and a Merganser? How do you tell if the bird you are watching is indeed a duck?

This book, like the earlier *Instant Guide to Birds*, will enable the reader and newcomer to birdwatching to identify positively and as simply as possible the great majority of birds found in and around inland water habitats. It provides a more detailed look at a broader selection of the species of birds you are likely to see around lakes, rivers, ponds, wet fields, marshes and bogs.

How to use this book

We have divided the book into nine sections, each indicated by a different color band at the top of the page (see Contents list on page 3.) These sections are: **Loons and Grebes; Herons and their allies; Waterfowl; Rails; Shorebirds; Gulls and Terns; Birds of Prey; Other Water Birds;** and **Water-related Species.**

Within each of these color-coded sections the birds are featured in ascending size order, the measurements given being from the point of the bill to the tip of the tail. Each size range is represented by a symbol (see Fig. 1) which is featured in the color band at the top of each page. To identify your bird, estimate its size and then decide to which section it belongs, using the *Guide to Identification* which follows.

Fig. 1 Guide to bird sizes

 Small
3¼–9½in

 Medium
10–15in

 Large
15½–27in

 Very large
28–62in

Additional information in this color band tells you whether the bird is a resident, a winter or summer visitor, or a migrant.

Guide to Identification

Page numbers given at the end of each section will enable you to turn directly to the relevant section of the book.

Loons and Grebes are fully aquatic birds. Their legs are placed towards the tail to provide strong propulsion for swimming and diving. They rarely visit land where they are ungainly and vulnerable. Their strongest characteristic is that they appear virtually tailless in flight, with large webbed feet trailing behind and a marked "drooped" head and neck. **14–19**

Herons and their allies are almost all larger species. Most are found wading in shallow water locations and are characterized by long legs and/or necks for their body size. Some winter at sea but all breed in trees or reed beds. **20–33**

Waterfowl include ducks, geese and swans — to most people probably the most familiar of water birds. They are birds of ponds, lakes and wetlands, feeding mainly on vegetation and frequently seen in large flocks. They are characterized by heavy bodies, flattened dabbling bills and pointed tails. **34–64**

Rails consist of a group of six species of skulking chicken-shaped birds, usually found in and around reed beds and water margins. Coots are the most adventurous and may be found on large bodies of open water. **65–70**

Shorebirds are a large and numerous group of birds found on and around water margins. Most have long legs for wading in shallow water and fairly long bills. They are rapid feeders, often in large flocks and this section contains many species with similar markings, often only seen at a distance across mud flats or estuaries. Careful observation is necessary to avoid confusion and make a positive identification. **71–99**

Gulls and Terns are very familiar "coastal" birds, frequently seen inland. Graceful and skilled in flight, their plumages almost invariably consist of combinations of gray, black and white, although bills and feet do vary. Plunge-divers and/or scavengers, these species are very visible when feeding. **100–110**

Birds of Prey: only two birds of prey rely on water habitats for survival. Both feed on fish and are very skilful and dramatic hunters. Talons and hooked beaks are used for holding and tearing their catch. **111–112**

Other Water Birds are three apparently unrelated species grouped together because they all depend on water for their food. The Dipper and the Kingfisher immerse themselves completely to secure their prey. All three species are found on free-flowing rivers and streams. **113–115**

Water-related Species: a section of birds which, although they are less dependent on water than the individually featured species, are closely associated with and need a wet habitat. They are grouped within the section by type of habitat (e.g. **Fields and Marsh**; **Wet Woodland**; **Streams etc.**).   116–121

Making a positive identification

Once you have decided on the section to which your bird belongs, you can turn to the pages on which the individual species are described and illustrated. Your estimate of size will be helpful at this point to locate the bird within its section.

In the first box of text on each page, you will find described the feature or combination of features that are unique to that bird in that size range. It may be that only one piece of information is necessary as with the "two prominent breast bands" of the Killdeer, or the "large orange throat pouch" of the Double-crested Cormorant. If you are certain of these features, which are also shown on the color illustration of each bird, then you have already made a positive identification and need read on only out of interest and to build up a more detailed picture of the bird.

If you are uncertain about these specific features, the second box completes the description and adds details for sexes and juveniles.

The third box deals with characteristic habits, range and habitat. The information on habitat and range can be used in conjunction with the distribution map featured for each bird.

Fig. 2 Distribution map

☐ **Summer** only

☐ **All year round**

☐ **Winter** only

Although the second and third boxes provide additional useful information, they do not specifically identify the particular bird. Only the first box can do that.

Lookalikes

The fourth box on each page gives the names of similar birds with which the featured bird could be confused. All these **Lookalikes** are either featured in detail themselves or appear in the final section of the book (Water-related species) grouped by habitat.

This Lookalikes box is important for two reasons. Firstly, it is very easy to jump to conclusions when looking for known identifying features. So check the Lookalikes carefully. Size is easily misjudged and buff plumage, for instance, often mistaken for yellow. This box will give you other possibilities to consider.

Secondly it is very important for the observer to be aware of exactly what points he should be looking for, as a means of quickly distinguishing similar birds. This is where guesswork ends and skill begins.

Now you are ready to use this book. It is designed to fit into your pocket, so take it with you on your next trip. Good birdwatching, and don't forget to check your sightings on the check-list provided with the index!

Fig. 3 Specimen page

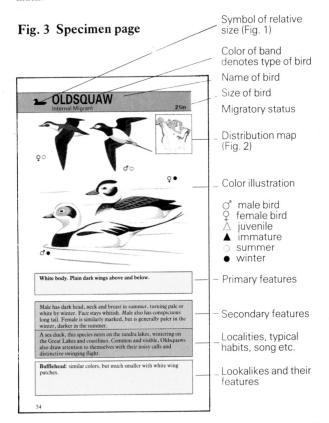

Symbol of relative size (Fig. 1)

Color of band denotes type of bird

Name of bird

Size of bird

Migratory status

Distribution map (Fig. 2)

Color illustration

♂ male bird
♀ female bird
△ juvenile
▲ immature
○ summer
● winter

Primary features

Secondary features

Localities, typical habits, song etc.

Lookalikes and their features

OLDSQUAW
Internal Migrant

21in

♀○

♂○

♀●

♂●

White body. Plain dark wings above and below.

Male has dark head, neck and breast in summer, turning pale or white by winter. Face stays whitish. Male also has conspicuous long tail. Female is similarly marked, but is generally paler in the winter, darker in the summer.

A sea duck, this species nests on the tundra lakes, wintering on the Great Lakes and coastlines. Common and visible, Oldsquaws also draw attention to themselves with their noisy calls and distinctive swinging flight.

Bufflehead: similar colors, but much smaller with white wing patches.

54

Glossary of terms

Adult A mature bird capable of breeding.

Bar A relatively narrow band of color across the area described, e.g. wing bars on Empidonax Flycatchers.

Call A few notes, or even a single note, indicating alarm or acting as a simple statement of presence.

Display A ritualized pattern of behavior, usually movement, by which birds communicate, particularly during courtship and in defense of territory.

Hybrid Interbreeding can sometimes occur between different but similar species, any offspring being hybrids, usually showing some aspects of plumage and behavior of each parent, e.g. Mallard and American Black Duck.

Immature A fully grown bird not yet old enough to breed, often in plumage markedly different from the adult.

Internal migrant Species present throughout the year within North America, but with the population showing consistent migration according to the seasons, e.g. Western Grebe.

Juvenile A young bird in its own first plumage variation, having left the nest but not completed its first molt at the end of summer.

Migratory Any species exhibiting movement consistent with the change of seasons is a migratory species.

Molt Change of plumage, usually before winter and before breeding.

Passage migrant A migratory species, usually seen briefly in spring and/or fall, en route to its breeding or wintering grounds, e.g. Pectoral Sandpiper.

Patch An area of color, perhaps on the cheek, e.g. Yellow-crowned Night-Heron.

Range That area which contains the vast proportion of the population of the species considered.

Resident Present throughout the year, e.g. Common Moorhen; the local population may be supplemented by partial migrants from adjoining areas.

Shield A structure, lacking feathers, on the forehead of some water birds, e.g. American Coot.

Song A sustained and consistent collection of notes used principally to proclaim ownership of territory, particularly during the breeding season.

Spatulate Having a long, spread and flattened shape, e.g. the bill of the Northern Shoveler.

Species A group of individuals (population) whose members resemble each other more closely than they resemble members of other populations and which, almost invariably, are capable of breeding only amongst themselves.

Speculum A panel on the trailing edge of the inner wing feathers of ducks, usually highly and distinctively colored, e.g. Mallard.

Stripe A relatively narrow, long band of color along the area described, e.g. wing stripe on a Spotted Sandpiper.

Subspecies A group of individuals within a species which differ slightly, usually in plumage, from the typical form but which are capable of breeding with any individual of that species.

Summer visitor A migratory species, arriving in spring and returning to its winter home at the end of the breeding season, e.g. Bank Swallow.

Winter visitor A migratory species, arriving in late fall and returning to its summer home to breed when conditions there improve in spring, e.g. Snow Goose.

Fig. 4 The parts of a bird

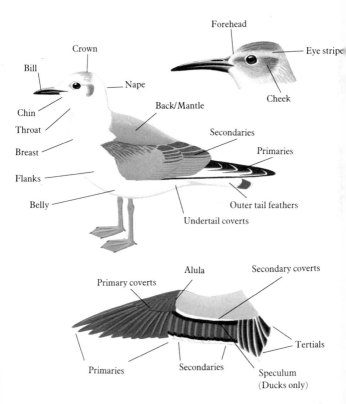

EARED GREBE
Resident/Internal Migrant

13in

Abrupt tail. **Summer:** colorful fanned ear tufts and black neck. **Winter:** dark ear coverts remain.

Slender uptilted lower bill tip distinctive when near. Summer: golden ear tufts contrast with black crested head and back; flanks are chestnut, underparts white. Winter: dark upperparts; whitish areas on face, neck and underparts remain.

Usually seen nesting in colonies in freshwater lakes, this attractive bird migrates to winter locations both inland and coastal. As with other grebes and divers, this species has a labored wing action with the typical drooped neck extended.

Horned Grebe: (summer) colorful ear tufts and chestnut neck, (winter) white ear coverts. **Pied-billed Grebe:** stocky with abrupt tail. Deep bill, encircled by a black ring in summer. Other **Grebes** (winter): far larger. All **Ducks** have flattened bills and pointed tails.

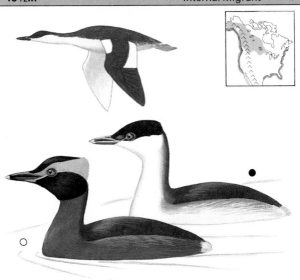

Tailless profile. **Summer: colorful ear tufts and chestnut neck. Winter: white cheeks and ear coverts.**

Straight-billed. In summer the tops of the ear tufts are gold, the lower parts dark like the back. The flanks are chestnut and the underparts white. In winter bright colors disappear and the front half of the neck becomes white.

It breeds on freshwater lakes and ponds, migrating mainly to coastal locations for the winter. Notice the way in which it leaps forward into dives, and the typical fast wing action with drooped neck extended in flight.

Eared Grebe: (summer) colorful ear tufts and black neck, (winter) dark ear coverts remain. **Pied-billed Grebe:** stocky with abrupt tail. Deep bill, encircled by a black ring in summer. Other **Grebes** (winter): far larger. All **Ducks** have flattened bills and pointed tails.

15

PIED-BILLED GREBE
Resident/Summer Visitor

13½in

Stocky profile with abrupt tail. Summer: deep pale bill encircled by a black ring. Winter: deep unmarked pale bill.

Summer: brown overall with black chin and pale belly. Winter: chin turns white, otherwise more rufous, especially neck. Juveniles are downy and heavily streaked.

Numerous on ponds, marshes and lakes, but not easily seen due to secretive nature. It has the ability to sink leaving only its head above water. Winters on salt water, coastal bays included.

Horned and **Eared Grebes**: fairly stocky profiles with slender bills and colorful ear tufts in summer. All **Ducks** have flattened bills and pointed tails.

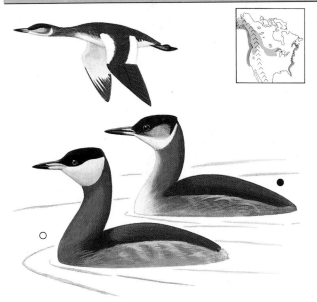

Dagger-like black and yellow bill. Summer: red neck and pale gray cheeks. Winter: dusky sides to neck and crescent pattern on face.

Dark forehead, crown, back of neck, back are same winter and summer, as are whitish underparts. Appears tailless. In flight, white wing patches on front and rear inner wing. Yellow on bill is duller in winter, but normally visible.

Secretive and not common, this species is to be found breeding in freshwater lakes and ponds. In winter it switches to coastal saltwater locations. Typical of grebes in flight, the drooped extended neck is a good identifying feature.

Western Grebe (winter): much larger with a long slim neck and slim yellow bill. Other **Grebes** (winter): far smaller with shorter bills. All **Ducks** have flattened bills and pointed tails.

WESTERN GREBE
Internal Migrant

Long, slim black and white neck. Slim yellow bill.

Dark gray-brown above. White below. In flight a single strong white wing stripe is visible. There are dark and light-faced color patterns of this same species.

Remarkable courtship behavior: both birds race across the water with drooped necks. Favors large open lakes in summer, mainly coasts in winter. Dark-faced northern birds give a two-note call, the southerly light-faced birds a single note.

Other **Grebes**: much smaller.

Black dagger-like bill, and glossy dark green head in summer.

Mostly pied plumage, a heavily checkered back, striped patch on neck, stripes into spots on flanks. White below, but other colors fade to gray in adult in winter and resemble immatures.

Loons have striking flight profiles, the neck and head being slung low. They are also noted for swimming low. Nest in wooded lakes giving remarkable yodeling call. Winter on the coast.

Mergansers: smaller, slim red bills. **Ducks**: smaller, flattened bills. **Cormorants**: hooked bills.

LEAST BITTERN
Resident/Summer Visitor

12½in

♂

Very small, the smallest heron-type with extensive buff area on inner forewing.

Crown, back, tail, primaries are brown/black. Buff wing areas are cinnamon-edged. Face, neck rust colored fading towards white belly. Neck shows streaking on adult female, more so on the juvenile. Bill is medium length, dagger-like.

These secretive little birds prefer freshwater marshes and overgrown shallow water locations. They creep around reed beds stalking prey, and freeze with the bill vertical when alarmed, flying at the last moment. Call is a low "cucucu."

American Bittern: far larger bird with mid-brown upperparts and black flight feathers which show well in flight. Immature **Green-backed Heron** and **Night-Herons**: far larger and lack buff wing markings. **Rails**: chicken shape, barred flanks.

Small heron with medium length bill. Adults have dark green back and chestnut neck, immatures have heavily streaked neck.

Dagger-like bill. Adults have dark green crowns with a crest, white down the front of the throat and underparts, and muddy-yellow legs. In flight the legs project well beyond the tail. Immatures have very dark brown backs.

Fairly common and widespread, this species is found in marshes, swamps, overgrown water margins and streams. It perches in trees. Normally a shy bird, it shows alarm by raising its crest and by flicking movements.

Adult: **Least Bittern**: smaller, shows buff on wings. Immature: **Night-Herons**: larger with shorter bills. Their more closely streaked necks contrast less with the rest of their plumage.

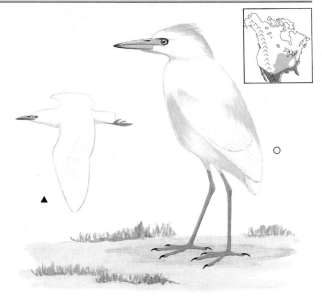

White heron-type with either orange or yellow bill and yellowish legs.

Slightly bulky in appearance, it becomes elegant during breeding when adorned with pale orange plumes on the head, lower neck and back. The bill becomes more orange-red and the legs redden. Immatures lack plumes and color changes.

An introduced species, thriving where there is livestock or cultivated land. It is now common, mostly in the South where it is resident. Summer visitors are now seen in most regions, often in quite large flocks. The wing action is rapid.

Snowy Egret: black bill and legs. Immature **Little Blue Heron**: gray bill tipped with black. Patches of gray especially at wing tips. **Great Egret**: far larger. Black legs. **Great White (Blue) Heron**: huge by comparison.

1

Remarkable downcurved bills, green and purple plumages.

From a distance these two species appear very dark all over, except for the white area at the base of the bill of the White-faced Ibis (**1**). Close to, the feathers are glossy and colorful. Winter and immature plumages of the two are alike.

Generally, these two species may be separated by their ranges, which barely overlap. Glossy Ibises prefer salt and freshwater marshes near the coast. White-faced Ibises markedly prefer freshwater locations, mostly inland, across the central U.S.

Whimbrel, Long-billed Curlew: striped and speckled brown plumages. Confusion only possible at a distance.

23

Upperparts are mid-brown, except for black flight feathers which show well in flight.

The underparts are buff with heavy brown streaks. Adults show a prominent black neck stripe, lacking in young birds. Note the pointed wings in flight. The bill is medium length and dagger-like.

This secretive bird prefers freshwater marshes and heavily overgrown shallow water locations. It creeps around reed beds stalking prey and freezes with the bill vertical. The call is a thumping "oong-ka-lunk." It is not seen in trees.

Immature **Green-backed Heron** and **Night-Herons**: similar size and shape, but back and upper wings are the same color. **Least Bittern**: far smaller with extensive buff area on the inner forewing.

Gray bill tipped with black. **Adult: whole body slate blue with purple neck. Immature: white all over.**

The purple neck of breeding birds becomes "plumed," the feathers not developing in non-breeding adults. The legs are a dark muddy color. Molting immature all-white birds start to develop the adult plumage, giving a "patchy" appearance.

Breeding birds are restricted to the southeast, but immatures may be seen widely through the continent in shallow water areas of marshes, ponds and coastal saltwater locations. Note the deliberate method of stalking food, unlike some similar species.

Adult: none. Immature: immature **Snowy Egret** has black bill. Adult **Snowy Egret** has black bill and yellow feet with black legs. **Cattle Egret**: orange-yellow bill. **Great Egret**: much larger with yellow bill and black legs. **Great White (Blue) Heron**: very much larger with yellow bill.

Black bill and legs, yellow feet.

Pure white. When breeding exhibits striking plumes from head, neck and back, the back plumes curling upwards. The feet become orange.

Plentiful in swamps, marshes and ponds shallow enough for it to wade. It disturbs its prey with its feet and then darts the dagger-shaped bill repeatedly into the water until the meal is secured.

Cattle Egret: orange-yellow bill. Yellowish legs which may redden when breeding. Immature **Little Blue Heron**: gray bill tipped black. Patches of gray, especially at wing tips. **Great White (Blue) Heron**: much larger, yellow legs. **Great Egret**: much larger, black feet.

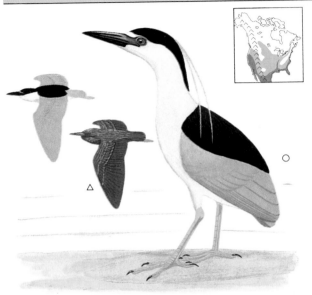

A stocky, short-legged heron. Adults have black crown and back. Immatures have a browner crown and back, heavily spotted with white in the juvenile.

Adults: whitish face, neck plumes, underparts. Gray wings and tail. Medium-short bill is all black, legs yellowish green. In flight little more than the feet project beyond the tail. Immatures: some yellow on lower bill, underparts streaky brown.

A bird of marshes, overgrown water margins, even cities, it is normally seen roosting in trees. Mostly nocturnal, it leaves to feed around dusk. Reasonably common it is seen widely across the U.S. as a visitor. Resident near coastlines.

Adult: **Yellow-crowned Night-Heron**: whitish crown and cheek patch. Immatures: **Yellow-crowned Night-Heron**: smaller white spots on upperparts, lower leg projects beyond tail in flight. **American Bittern**: black flight feathers. **Green-backed Heron**: smaller. Longer bill. Legs project in flight.

27

Stocky, medium-legged heron. Adults have whitish crown and cheek patch. Immatures are more gray-brown in coloring with small white spots on upperparts.

Adults have the remainder of the head black with all other plumage gray. The medium-short bill is black, the legs orange-yellow. In flight the feet and lower legs project beyond the tail. Immature birds have streaked upperparts.

A bird of marshes, mangrove swamps and wet areas with trees, in which they roost, this is predominantly an eastern species. Its range extends from Florida and the southern coastal areas where it is resident, northwards to the Great Lakes in summer.

Adults: **Black-crowned Night-Heron**: black crown and back.
Immatures: **Black-crowned Night-Heron**: heavier white spots on upperparts, feet only project beyond tail in flight. **American Bittern**: black flight feathers. **Green-backed Heron**: smaller. Longer bill. Heavily streaked neck. Legs project in flight.

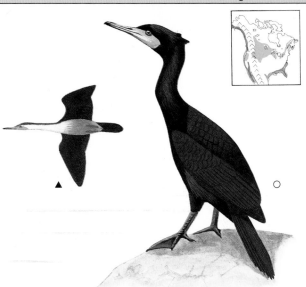

Large orange throat pouch.

Plumage is very green overall. The crests vary, being whitish in the west, dark in the east. Immature birds are brown above, paler below.

Widespread, often seen in numbers in flight with characteristic head up, bent-necked attitude. They swim low in the water and emerge to dry out with spread wings. Common coastally and inland around any major body of water.

Common Loon: black dagger-like bill, glossy dark green head without pouch. **Anhinga**: long snaky neck and disproportionately long tail.

29

ANHINGA
Resident/Summer Visitor

34in

♀

♂

♂○

Long snaky neck, and disproportionately long tail.

The bird has predominantly dark glossy green body plumage with very visible silvery white wing patches. The head and neck of the male is also glossy green, that of the female buff-brown. Immatures are brownish overall.

At rest, Anhingas perch with wings outspread. In flight they flap slowly, the long neck outstretched. When swimming, they are able to submerge the body with only the neck above water. Favor swamps, freshwater locations in the southeastern U.S.

Double-crested Cormorant: large orange throat pouch.

Yellow dagger-like bill, long black legs and feet.

Pure white. When breeding, it trails long straight plumes from back and neck.

Found in swamps, marshes, ponds and mud flats shallow enough for it to wade, it hunts its prey stealthily, leaning forward, quite unlike the smaller Snowy Egret.

Great White (Blue) Heron: yellow legs and feet. **Snowy Egret**: smaller, black bill and yellow feet. **Cattle Egret**: smaller, yellow legs which may redden when breeding. Immature **Little Blue Heron**: smaller, gray bill tipped black. Patches of gray, especially at wing tips.

Long black-streaked neck and black eyebrow stripe to crest.

The white head, blue-gray back and wings (much darker trailing edge and primaries,) yellow dagger bill and long yellow legs make this a very distinctive species. The "Great White Heron" of Florida is an all-white subspecies with yellow legs.

Mainly solitary, it frequents most wet habitats, spearing fish from the shallows. In flight, slow wingbeats and neck tucked back make this an elegant bird.

Sandhill Crane: untidy "bustle" at rear overhangs the tail feathers. Great White Heron: subspecies is far larger than all other white heron-types except the Great Egret, which has black rather than yellow legs.

Extremely large white bird, with a huge orange bill (gray in immature.)

White all over except for black primaries and outer secondaries, with bright orange feet to match the bill. Breeding birds show a "flag" midway down the upper bill. Immature birds have gray on head and neck.

A sociable species; flocks may be seen on lakes fishing by dipping their bills in unison, scooping up fish in their remarkable throat pouches. Flight is deliberate but powerful with much gliding. Migration is unpredictable but widespread.

Swans, Geese, Herons, Egrets and **Ibises** with white plumage are all large birds, but are quite different at close range. All lack the huge orange bill.

Small, puffy-headed duck: the male has a large white triangle over the back of the head, the female has a white cheek patch.

White wing patches visible in flight on dark wings and back. Male has a white body, breast and neck. The remainder of the head is black. Female has a brown head with gray back and dusky flanks.

Buffleheads migrate from nesting grounds on wooded lakes and ponds in Canada and the north, down to inland and coastal waters in the winter. This species is widespread and reasonably common.

Hooded Merganser: long, slim bill. **Goldeneyes**: larger, with males showing white head patch before the eye. **Oldsquaw**: larger, plain dark wings. **Ruddy Duck**: plain wings.

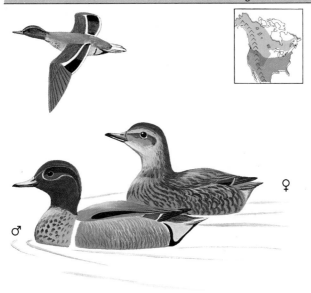

Small size, green speculum, brown forewing.

Male has chestnut and green head, gray sides with a clearly visible vertical white stripe, a speckled breast and a prominent buff patch beneath the tail. The female is a uniform mottled brown.

This small dabbling duck feeds mainly on aquatic plants in freshwater locations. It nests on the ground. It is notable for its agile flight, often in large flocks, and for the vertical take-off from water when disturbed. Common.

Blue-winged Teal: larger, blue forewing. **American Wigeon**: larger, white forewing. **Ruddy Duck, Bufflehead**: similar size but different shape with white on head.

♀

♂

Small size and stiff tail.

Very distinctive shape with head too big for body. When breeding, male shows very white face, blue bill, dark crown and ruddy body. Female lacks ruddy color, shows brown cheek stripe. Colors fade in winter, but male retains white face.

This active little duck is common, gregarious and usually seen on large bodies of water. It has a rapid flight and no markings on the upper wing, very unusual in a duck. If alarmed, it will dive immediately.

None.

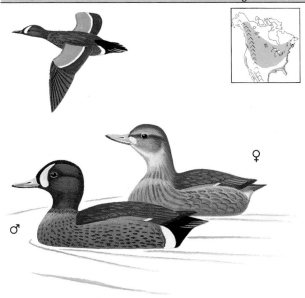

♀

♂

Small size, blue forewing. Male has white crescent on face. Both sexes have a smaller bill than Cinnamon Teal.

Male has a dark gray head and neck, black and white undertail, strongly spotted flanks and breast, and a green speculum which he shares with the mottled brown female. The female strongly resembles Cinnamon Teal but is grayer.

Broadly distributed in the summer, this species is usually seen on lakes, marshes and ponds. Agile in flight, the blue forewing may appear whitish. Winters mainly in Peru and Uruguay.

Northern Shoveler: pale blue forewing, spatulate bill. **Green-winged Teal**: similar size, lacks blue forewing. Female **Cinnamon Teal**: almost no facial markings, longer moderately spatulate bill.

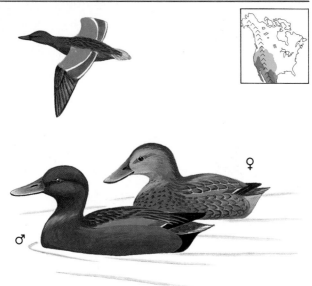

CINNAMON TEAL

Internal Migrant

16in

♀

♂

Small size, blue forewing. Male cinnamon-colored. Both sexes have a moderately spatulate bill, longer than that of Blue-winged Teal. Note restricted western range.

Green speculum. Mottled brown back. Female is a uniform mottled brown and rather darker than the female Blue-winged Teal.

Very much restricted to the west. Its usual habitats are lakes, marshes and ponds. It associates with, and sometimes interbreeds with, the very similar Blue-winged Teal.

Northern Shoveler: larger bird, longer fully spatulate bill, male has green head, female bill is orange-edged. **Blue-winged Teal**: same wing marking, but male distinct, female shows an eye stripe and has a shorter non-spatulate bill.

♀

♂

Peaked head. White band around dark bill.

Broad pale gray stripe on trailing wing edges. Male has very dark head, neck, breast and back, with pale gray flanks preceded by prominent white vertical band. White at bill base may be visible. Female mostly brown with pale chin and white eye stripe.

Fairly common on wooded lakes and ponds, in winter it extends into marshes, rivers and bays. Breeding mostly in Canada, it migrates south to southern states and Mexico, but has a very variable range.

Both **Scaups**: plain bills; male: white flanks, female: prominent white area around base of bill. **Redhead**: male: pale-backed, female: gray-blue bill, tipped black. **Canvasback**: very pale back.

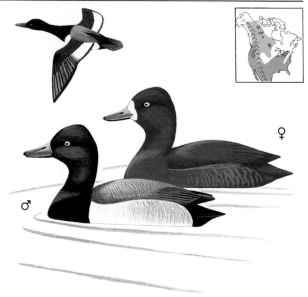

Broad white stripe along trailing upper wing diminishing in primaries. Peaked head, plain bill with a black tip.

Similar to Greater Scaup, but male's head and neck dark purple. Black breast, undertail, grayish-white flanks and gray back. Female is brown overall with white at base of bill and on belly. Both sexes have gray bill tipped black.

Highly migratory and common, this species is seen on most water habitats. It breeds all across the northwest, and in winter is visible in flocks, often with Greater Scaup, on lakes, ponds and bays.

Greater Scaup: rounded head, white stripe along length of trailing upper wing. Male has all white flanks. **Ring-necked Duck**: white band around dark bill. **Canvasback, Redhead**: males have chestnut heads, females lack white at base of bill.

Small ducks, very dark overall, with no visible speculum.

Stocky build with steep forehead and stubby bills. Male has scattered white areas on otherwise slate blue plumage, with dark red flanks. Female is brown with white "ear patch" and face markings. Pale belly.

A sea duck, this species nests alongside mountain streams, where it can be seen regularly on migration to its coastal wintering grounds. Here it favors rocky locations in heavy surf. Not gregarious, and does not mix with other species.

White-winged Scoter: much larger, white speculum, larger bill.
Bufflehead: female very small, white on inner wing.

Long, slim gray bill. Both sexes have loose fan-shaped crest.

Pale-bellied, dark-backed, dark-winged ducks with black and white secondaries. Male has black and white head, neck and breast. Brown flanks. Female is gray-brown.

Not particularly common, this small Merganser favors wooded rivers and lakes for breeding. It shares the Merganser serrated bill and all-in-a-line (bill, head, body, tail) flight posture. In winter it is normally found inland.

Common, Red-breasted Mergansers: larger with red bills. Females: light-breasted. Other **Ducks** do not share long, slim bill.

♀

♂

Crested head and blue speculum.

Male: dark and irridescent above. Patterned green head, white collar, wine-red undertail coverts and breast, golden flanks, white belly. Female: teardrop-shaped eye patch. Otherwise dark brown, streaked below with a white belly.

A perching duck often seen doing just that quite high in trees where it nests. The trees need to be close to marshes, ponds or rivers. Call is a penetrating "hoo-eek."

Mallard: blue speculum edged with white on both sides. **Northern Shoveler**: green speculum and spatulate bill. **Red-breasted Merganser**: white speculum and crested head. **Green-winged Teal**: a small duck with a green speculum. Other female **Ducks** lack crest and white teardrop eye patch.

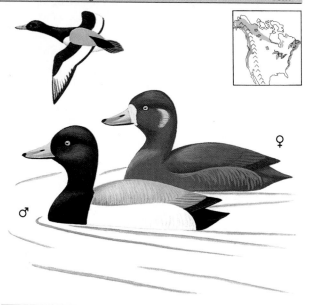

♀

♂

Broad white stripe all along trailing upper wing. Rounded head.

Similar to Lesser Scaup, but male's head and neck very dark green. Black breast, undertail, white flanks and gray back. Female is brown overall with white at base of bill and on belly. Both sexes have a plain gray bill, tipped black.

Highly migratory, this less common of the two Scaups nests on Canadian Tundra, but is visible in considerable numbers throughout migration on large lakes and bays. Often mixes with Lesser Scaups. A diving species.

Lesser Scaup: peaked head. White wing stripe diminishes in primaries. Male has grayer flanks. **Ring-necked Duck:** white band around dark bill. **Canvasback, Redhead:** males have chestnut heads, females lack white at base of bill.

Large white patch on forewing in front of a green speculum.

Male has a white crown, a green mask and mottled gray neck. He shares a blue bill and a predominantly brownish body with the female, but her whole head and neck are mottled gray.

A surface-feeding duck of shallow waters; large numbers may be seen on lakes, marshes and in fields. The name of Baldpate stems from the white cap and forehead of the male bird.

Other female marsh ducks lack white forewing patch. **Northern Pintail**: also notably larger. The **Gadwall** has a prominent white speculum.

Round-headed duck with a gray-blue bill, tipped black. Male has chestnut head and mid-gray back. Female is brown overall with a darker crown.

Male has pale gray flanks, and a black breast and undertail. Both sexes share an indistinct gray stripe on the trailing wing edges.

A diving duck, it eats mainly vegetable and some animal matter. In summer it breeds mainly in marshes. Highly migratory, it has a large range and may be seen on most large bodies of water.

Canvasback: long, triangular head and dark bill. Female has a pale back. **Ring-necked Duck**: female has white eye stripe and white band round a dark bill. **Scaups**: females have prominent white markings at base of pale bills. Males have very dark heads.

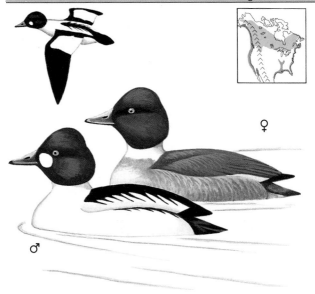

♀

♂

Male: white face spot on green head. Female: dark brown triangular head, white neck, gray bill tipped with yellow.

Gray wings with square white wing patches very visible in flight. Male has an almost black back and tail with very white underparts. Female has dark tail, gray flanks, white belly.

A sea duck, it summers on lakes, building its nest in nearby trees. Winter is spent either on the coast or large areas of inland water. Excellent diver: observers sometimes lose track of the bird as it travels great distances under water.

Barrow's Goldeneye male: purple head with crescent-shaped white spot. Female: very similar — but adult's bill is all yellow, forehead is steep. **Bufflehead**: smaller, white face patch behind eye. **Common Merganser**: long, slim bill.

47

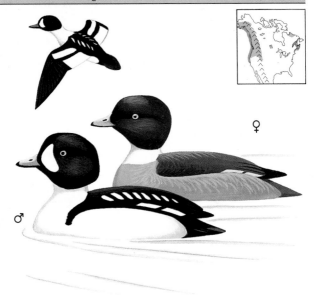

♀

♂

Male: white crescent on purple head. Female: dark brown head with steep forehead, white neck, bill yellow in adult.

Dark wings with double white wing patches visible in flight. Male has an almost black back and tail with very white underparts. Female has dark tail, gray-brown flanks and white belly.

A sea duck, it summers on lakes, nesting in trees nearby. Winter is spent on coasts or inland water. Excellent diver: observers may lose track as it travels great distances under water. A more restricted range than Common Goldeneye.

Common Goldeneye: head is triangular. Male: green head with white face spot before eye. Female: very similar but yellow-tipped gray bill and double white wing bars. **Bufflehead**: smaller, pale patch behind eye. **Common Merganser**: long, slim bill.

Unusually uniform, the gray drake and brown duck share a pale brown head and white speculum.

The male has a gray bill, white belly, black tail and some chestnut in the forewing. The female has a white belly, and the gray bill is edged with orange.

A shy species, Gadwall prefer quiet locations. Numerous on freshwater lakes and marshes, it is more common in the west.

Both **Scaup** have darker bodies with broad white wing bands. **Northern Pintail**, **Canvasback** and **Redhead** lack white speculum. Other **Ducks** have very dark or colorful plumage.

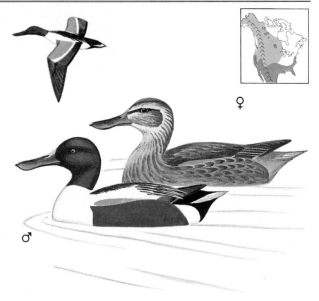

♀

♂

Large duck, distinctive long spatulate bill, orange-edged on female.

The sexes share a green speculum and a pale blue forewing. The male has a green head, white breast and tail tip, chestnut flanks and belly, black undertail and rump. The female is a uniform mottled brown.

Swims rapidly with head held low filtering plant food from the water. When disturbed it rises vertically from the water. This species favors ponds and marshes where the water is shallow and muddy.

Mallard has a blue speculum. **Red-breasted Merganser** has a white speculum. Any similar female is easily distinguished by the lack of long spatulate bill except **Cinnamon Teal**: smaller moderately spatulate bill. Note restricted western range.

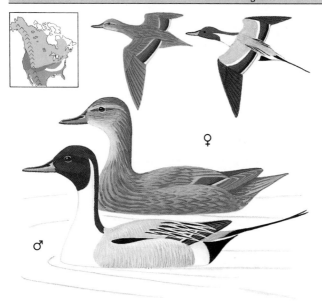

Long slender neck and gray bill; male with a long needle-tail, female's shorter.

Brown-winged. Brown speculum, edged white. Male: chocolate-brown head with a divider of white rising from the breast, gray back, black undertail coverts. Female: predominantly brown, white belly.

Widespread on most areas of water, it is frequently seen in numbers, grazing socially in fields. A shy bird, it disturbs easily. Very rapid flight action.

Female **Ruddy Duck**: smaller, short-necked. Other female **Ducks**: black slender neck and form.

CANVASBACK
Internal Migrant

21in

♀

♂

Very pale-backed duck with long triangular forehead and bill.

Pale flanks and dark bill shared by both sexes. The male has a chestnut head and neck, a black breast and undertail. The female and male during molt have a brown head, neck and breast.

A diving duck, it eats mostly vegetable matter with some worms, frogs etc. Seen in large flocks on open water, such as lakes and marshes. Very widespread, it breeds as far north as Alaska, wintering in Mexico and the south.

Redhead: similar marking but head shape is rounder, bill is stubbier and gray, tipped with black. **Ring-necked Duck**: dark back with a dome-shaped head. Both **Scaups**: shorter pale bills, head shapes more rounded.

52

Very dark duck overall, with white secondaries.

Heavily built sea-going shape. Underwings are pale. Otherwise the male is all black except for a white patch by the eye, the female is brown. When swimming, the white secondaries are visible as a patch towards the tail.

A sea duck, it nests on the tundra and inland lakes, and is highly visible on migration to its coastal wintering ground. Usually seen in flocks, this species dives for food, both animal and vegetable.

Harlequin Duck: much smaller, female has no visible speculum. **American Black Duck**: different shape, blue speculum.

OLDSQUAW
Internal Migrant

21in

♀○

♂○

♀●

♂●

White body. Plain dark wings above and below.

Male has dark head, neck and breast in summer, turning pale or white by winter. Face stays whitish. Male also has conspicuous long tail. Female is similarly marked, but is generally paler in the winter, darker in the summer.

A sea duck, this species nests on the tundra lakes, wintering on the Great Lakes and coastlines. Common and visible, Oldsquaws also draw attention to themselves with their noisy calls and distinctive swinging flight.

Bufflehead: similar colors, but much smaller with white wing patches.

♀

♂

Blue speculum edged white on both sides.

Male has yellow bill, glossy green head and neck. White collar and outer tail, chestnut breast, gray back and wings. Black curled tail feathers. Female has orange bill, whitish tail. Other plumage is a mixture of browns and buffs.

Both common and widespread, the Mallard is likely to be found surface feeding on any slow-moving freshwater body. Much domesticated, there are numerous varieties including the pure white.

Northern Shoveler: similar, but green speculum, spatulate bill. **American Black Duck**: violet speculum, edged white at rear only, if visible. **Wood Duck**: bluish speculum, crested head. **Red-breasted Merganser**: white speculum, crested head.

Very dark-bodied duck with a violet speculum.

Both sexes are virtually all brown. The head and neck are paler, and the female is consistently lighter than the male. The underwing is distinctively white in flight. Male has a yellow bill, female a green bill.

A wide habitat range from marshes and streams to lakes, rivers and estuaries. Interbreeding with the thriving Mallard population is producing greater numbers of hybrids.

Mallard: blue speculum edged white on both sides. **White-winged Scoter**: different habitat, different shape, white speculum.

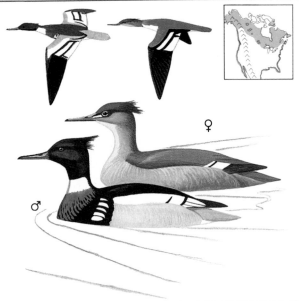

♀

♂

Long, slim red bill. Both sexes have twin-pronged crests.
Female's chin and front of throat are pale.

Male: glossy green head, white collar and rufous streaked breast.
Black above. Female: gray above with a rust-colored head. Both
sexes have gray wings and tail with pale underwing and belly.

This species nests in wooded areas around northern lakes, but in
winter migrates and may be seen on any body of water, fresh or
salt, including sea coasts. Distinctive all-in-a-line (bill, head,
body, tail) flight posture.

Common Merganser male: white breast and flanks. Female:
chestnut neck contrasts with white chin, white breast. **Hooded
Merganser**: smaller, loose crest. Female: dark-breasted. Other
Ducks do not share long, slim bill.

♀

♂

Long, slim red bill. Male: green head, rosy white breast.
Female: chestnut neck contrasts with white chin, rosy white
breast.

Gray wings with white secondaries, pale underwing and belly.
Male: white flanks. Female: chestnut head is crested. Gray flanks.

Very widespread, this species, mostly freshwater, nests in holes in
trees by lakes, rivers. The bill is serrated for holding fish. In
winter, flocks on large bodies of water. Distinctive all-in-a-line
(bill, head, body, tail) flight posture.

Red-breasted Merganser: double crest. Male: streaked breast.
Female: chin, front of throat and breast continuously pale.
Hooded Merganser: smaller, loose crest. Female: dark-breasted.
Other Ducks do not share long, slim bill.

Goose with white "chinstrap" and brown back.

Black head and neck. Brown wings and belly. Pale breast, white undertail and uppertail coverts. Black lower tail. Several subspecies with size decreasing northwards.

Our commonest goose. Widespread and often seen in flight in V-formation. Call is a noisy honking. Familiar on even quite small ponds, it settles on almost any body of water, and grazes on wetlands and fields in numbers.

Snow Goose: only similar in "blue phase" when whole head is white with gray-brown back. **Greater White-fronted Goose**: orange legs and feet. White margin around base of bill.

Orange legs and feet. White margin around base of bill of adults.

Head, neck and body are gray-brown. undertail is white. The bill is variable in color, either pink, or orange (Greenland race.) The breast and belly show strong irregular barring. Only the immature bird lacks white around the bill.

Freshwater geese, breeding across Canadian, Alaskan tundra. They migrate in large numbers giving a "laughing" call, overwintering widely throughout the U.S., in wet fields, marshes and lakes. Food consists largely of grasses.

Canada Goose: white "chinstrap," black feet. "Blue phase"
Snow Goose: pied goose with "grinning" pink bill.

Pied goose with "grinning" pink bill.

"White phase" is all white with just the primaries black. "Blue phase" has head and tail white, wing coverts blue-gray with the body and wings very dark. Immatures are brownish versions of each subspecies.

This species actually breeds on the Arctic tundra, but is widely seen on migration south. It winters on the Gulf coast in abundance, frequently with the two color phases together. Originally thought to be two separate species.

Greater White-fronted Goose: orange legs and feet. White margin around base of bill. Domestic **Geese** are all white with orange bills. **Swans** are all white and far larger.

Swan with slightly concave bill, black in adult, pinkish in immature. Round-shaped head.

This large bird is all white except for the black bill, the black and yellow skin between bill and eye, black legs and feet. In "Bewick's" subspecies (west only,) the yellow extends to the base of the bill. Immatures are "dirty" white.

Breeds on tundra, migrating across continent to wintering grounds on lakes, rivers, estuaries. Previously named "Whistling Swan" after noise of its wingbeat, not its high-pitched cry. Not very common, but the most numerous native swan.

Trumpeter Swan: straight bill. Triangular shaped head. **Mute Swan**: neck held in S-shape. Adult's bill is orange-red with knob at base. Immature has gray bill. **Snow Goose**: smaller, black primaries. White **Herons** and **Egrets** have long legs.

Swan with straight bill, black in adult, pinkish in immature.
Triangular shaped head.

All white except for the bill, the black skin between the bill and
eye and black legs and feet. The "Whooper" subspecies (west
only) has yellow from the eye deep into the bill. Immatures are a
"dirty" white.

Breeds locally in Canada, Alaska, northern U.S.A. Tends to
winter coastally in west on lakes, marshes, but currently in low
numbers. Normal call is a honk. Often bends base of neck back
sharply, with neck above erect.

Tundra Swan: slightly concave bill. Round head shape. **Mute
Swan**: neck held in S-shape. Adult's bill is orange-red with knob
at base. Immature has gray bill. **Snow Goose**: smaller, black
primaries. White **Herons** and **Egrets** have long legs.

MUTE SWAN
Resident

Neck held in S-shape. Adult has orange-red bill with knob at base. Immature's bill is gray.

All white except for the bill, black knob and skin between the bill and eye, black legs and feet. The knob is larger on the male bird and absent on the juvenile, which has dingy gray plumage. The tail is slightly cocked.

An introduced Swan, the graceful bird of parks, with the habit of arching its wings over its back to show aggression. In flight, noisy throbbing wingbeats are heard from a distance. Otherwise almost silent, hence the name.

Tundra Swan: slightly concave bill. Round head shape.
Trumpeter Swan: straight bill. Triangular head shape. **Snow Goose**: smaller, black primaries. White **Herons** and **Egrets** have long legs.

Barred flanks, long bill, small size.

Similar to small brown chicken with a long bill, the adults have brown backs streaked with black, wings and underparts are chestnut, face is gray, legs and bill are red. Juveniles are brownish black.

Common in fresh and saltwater marshes, the secretive nature of rails can make these birds an elusive sighting. Strongly migratory, their flight is reluctant, with legs dangling. They creep through cover giving harsh "kidick" cries.

King Rail: much larger. **Sora**: short-billed. **Common Moorhen**, **American Coot**: plain, very dark plumage.

△

Barred flanks, short bill.

Similar to a small brown chicken, the adults have brown backs streaked with black, the gray neck is black-throated, the bill and legs are greenish yellow. Juveniles are brown-throated.

Common in grain fields, fresh and saltmarshes, their secretive nature can make sightings difficult. Strongly migratory, flight is awkward and reluctant. Good swimmers, they creep in cover giving the cry, "ker-wee."

Virginia and **King Rails**: long-billed. **Common Moorhen, American Coot**: plain, very dark plumage.

Head, neck and underparts deep purple.

Red bill tipped yellow, pale blue forehead shield, green-brown back, prominent white undertail and noticeably yellow legs. Sexes alike. Juveniles are brown above, sandy below.

Common locally in southeastern areas, it is found in freshwater swamps and marshes. It is a highly migratory species wintering as far south as South America.

American Coot: whitish bill and small red forehead shield. **Common Moorhen**: white flank stripes. **Sora** and other **Rails** have barred flanks.

White flank stripe.

Though often appearing black, the back plumage is dark brown. The yellow-tipped red bill and shield are very distinctive, as are the white outer undertail coverts.

Favors a variety of freshwater habitats from marshes and small ponds to rivers. Easily disturbed, it shows alarm by flicking its tail to display white outer feathers.

American Coot: white bill and small red forehead shield. **Purple Gallinule**: pale blue shield, purple head and underparts. **Ducks** have larger flattened bills.

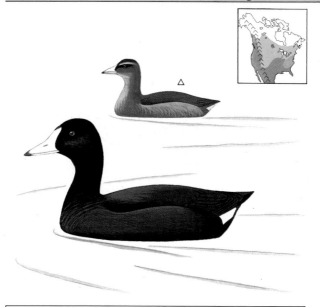

Whitish bill and small red forehead shield.

Black head and neck. Dark gray elsewhere except for white on the outer undertail coverts. Has most improbable lobe-webbed feet.

More aquatic than the moorhen, coots favor wide stretches of open water in addition to marshes and ponds, including salt bays. Gregarious birds, they often flock in winter. Labored fliers, they skitter along water to get airborne.

Common Moorhen: white flank stripe, yellow-tipped red bill.
Purple Gallinule: pale blue shield, purple head and underparts.
Ducks have larger flattened bills.

Barred flanks, long bill, large size.

Similar to a brown chicken with a long bill, the adults have brown backs streaked with black, underparts and cheeks are rusty red. Juveniles are less rusty with paler underparts.

Common in freshwater marshes and swamps, some are found in saltwater locations in winter. However, as with other rails, this species is rarely seen, the repeated "kek" call being the indication that they are present.

Sora, Virginia Rail: much smaller. Common Moorhen, American Coot: plain, very dark plumage.

SEMIPALMATED SANDPIPER

6in   Summer Visitor/Passage Migrant

Very small shorebird with black legs, a short solid bill, and white rump divided by black.

Brown "scaly" back plumage, closely streaked crown, neck and upper breast, plain white undertail, belly and flanks. Juveniles are generally darker above with a prominent white eyebrow stripe. Winter plumage paler, back less scaly.

The commonest "Peep" Sandpiper, seen widely inland on migration. Far more frequent in the east than the west, some birds overwinter in Florida, but most migrate on into South America. Call-note lacks "eee" of other "Peeps."

Other **"Peep" Sandpipers**: see their primary features. Other **Sandpipers**: **Solitary**: dark back, barred rump. (Winter) **Common**: olive back, saddle mark. **Stilt**: long legs. **Pectoral**: breast/belly contrast, yellowish legs. (Winter) **Red Knot**: stout, pale "scaly" back. **Sanderling**: behavior pattern.

Very small shorebird with muddy-yellow legs, a short fine bill, and white rump divided by black.

Very dark brown "scaly" back plumage, closely streaked crown, neck and all of breast, plain white undertail, belly and flanks. Juveniles have strong breast markings and winter birds generally have paler plumage.

This is the smallest "Peep" Sandpiper, regularly seen on migration, in marshes, pools and particularly mud flats. Breeding in Alaska, Canada, this species overwinters in the southern U.S. and South America. The usual note is "kreeep."

Other "Peep" Sandpipers: see their primary features. Other **Sandpipers: Solitary**: dark back, barred rump. (Winter) **Common**: olive back, saddle mark. **Stilt**: long legs. **Pectoral**: breast/belly contrast. (Winter) **Red Knot**: stout, pale "scaly" back. (Winter) **Sanderling**: behavior pattern.

Very small shorebird with black legs, a medium length slightly downcurved bill and white rump divided by black.

Brown "scaly" back plumage, closely streaked crown, neck and breast, spotting on flanks, and rufous coloring around the crown and ears. Juveniles lack the rufous color and flank spots. Winter plumage is very pale, back less "scaly."

A "Peep" Sandpiper, this common species is seen widely inland on migration. An Arctic breeder, it overwinters on southern coasts as well as in South America, rare for the similar Semipalmated Sandpiper. Call-note is "jeet."

Other **"Peep" Sandpipers**: see their primary features. Other **Sandpipers**: **Solitary**: dark back, barred rump. (Winter) **Common**: olive back, saddle mark. **Stilt**: long legs. **Pectoral**: breast/belly contrast, yellowish legs. (Winter) **Red Knot**: stout, pale "scaly" back. (Winter) **Sanderling**: behavior pattern.

♂ ○

Single breast band, orange legs, medium brown back.

The stubby bill is orange, tipped with black. The crown and nape match the back, the forehead matches the breast band, the remaining plumage is white. The sexes are alike. Winter colors fade a little, although the bill darkens.

This species breeds in the far north. Widespread during migration, it may be seen throughout the continent. Wintering grounds are mostly on mud flats, sand bars and beaches.

Killdeer: two prominent black breast bands. Other Shorebirds of a similar size are likely to be confused only in flight, but the noticeably longer bills will distinguish them.

74

SPOTTED SANDPIPER

Internal Migrant

Summer: striking round spots on underparts. Winter: light brown "saddle" mark across neck.

Olive brown plumage above, white below. When breeding, adults have barred upperparts. A white wing stripe is visible in flight, as are black and white outer tail feathers. Black eye stripe, white eyebrow stripe.

Widespread and commonest of sandpipers, it is normally seen in the summer on inland waterways. It has a stuttering flight on stiff wings. On the ground, it bobs and teeters uncertainly. It winters in the south and South America.

(Summer) other **Shorebirds**: spots not round and rarely on belly. (Winter) **Stilt Sandpiper**: long legs and bill. Other **Sandpipers**: plain olive-green back distinguishes as all others have dark backs or are heavily flecked with black. **Plovers**: all have stubby bills.

WHITE-RUMPED SANDPIPER
Passage Migrant   7½in

Small shorebird with black legs, the white rump is undivided,
and the folded wings project beyond the tail.

Brown "scaly" back plumage, closely streaked crown, neck,
breast and flanks with a plain white undertail and belly. Quite
rufous in breeding plumage, returning birds are grayer in fall,
juvenile and winter plumages much less spotted.

Not very common, this "Peep" Sandpiper is seen on migration
mainly in marshes and on mud flats. Wintering only in South
America it migrates from summer breeding grounds in the Arctic
tundra. Normal call-note is a squeaky "jeet."

Other "**Peep**" **Sandpipers**: see their primary features. Other
Sandpipers: **Solitary**: dark back, barred rump. (Winter)
Common: olive back, saddle mark. **Stilt**: long legs. **Pectoral**:
breast/belly contrast, yellowish legs. (Winter) **Red Knot**: stout,
pale "scaly" back. (Winter) **Sanderling**: behavior pattern.

Small shorebird with black legs, the white rump divided by dark brown, and folded wings projecting beyond the tail.

Brown "scaly" back plumage, closely streaked buff crown, neck and breast with plain white belly and flanks. Juveniles appear even more "scaly"-backed.

A "Peep" Sandpiper, not particularly common, seen on migration inland in wet fields, small pools, ponds, and on mud flats. Wintering only in South America, it is seen normally in summer and juvenile plumages. Call-note is "kreep."

Other "**Peep**" **Sandpipers**: see their primary features. Other **Sandpipers**: **Solitary**: dark back, barred rump. (Winter) **Common**: olive back, saddle mark. **Stilt**: long legs. **Pectoral**: breast/belly contrast, yellowish legs. (Winter) **Red Knot**: stout, pale "scaly" back. (Winter) **Sanderling**: behavior pattern.

Remarkable scuttling run at water's edge, back and forth with the waves.

Usually seen around freshwater as juveniles (illustrated) or molting adults, they are scaly-backed, in contrast to the plain pale gray of the winter adult. In summer the whole front half of the bird is uniformly rust colored.

In summer it breeds on the Arctic tundra. In winter we see it around the Great Lakes and on sandy beaches all around the shorelines, feeding in between the waves. This high activity makes the species distinctive.

No other shorebirds feed running with the waves, but note: **Red Knot**: larger, pale wings with poorly defined wing stripe. (Winter) **Dunlin**: downcurved bill. **Sandpipers**: wing stripes are poorly defined.

SOLITARY SANDPIPER

In flight, note that white rump and tail are divided by a black stripe and crossed by heavy black bars.

The dark brown back and wings are seen as unmarked in flight. Head, breast and sides are streaked, underparts white. The bill is slender, legs are olive green, eye rim white. The whiter-throated juvenile is illustrated.

Basically a summer visitor to Canada and Alaska, it migrates through the continent. Some birds overwinter in the southernmost states of the U.S. Widely seen on marshes, ponds, streamsides, often bobbing agitatedly.

Spotted Sandpiper: poorly defined wing stripe. **Semipalmated, Pectoral, Western, Least** and **Baird's Sandpipers** have divided rumps but lack the cross bars. **Lesser Yellowlegs, Stilt** and **White-rumped Sandpipers** have undivided white rump. **Greater Yellowlegs, Dowitchers**: larger, undivided white rump.

STILT SANDPIPER
Internal Migrant

8½in

Long green legs. White rump, not divided, and a dark back.

Long, slightly downcurved bill. Buff colored face, neck and pale breast; belly covered with dark brown stripes and bars respectively. Prominent eye stripe chestnut-edged during breeding. Juvenile, and winter plumages, plainer.

Feeding like the Dowitchers with a "stitching" action, it is often seen in their company on mud flats and marshes. An Arctic breeder, it winters in South America and so is seen on migration, spring and fall.

Dowitchers: larger, white wedge up the dark back. **Yellowlegs, Wilson's Phalarope** (winter): yellow legs. **Red Knot, Common Snipe**: larger, heavier build, with average length legs. **Solitary Sandpiper**: white rump and tail divided by a black stripe and crossed by heavy black bars.

Long, slightly downcurved bill. **Summer:** black belly. **Winter:**
unpatterned gray-brown back.

Stocky build. In summer, chestnut brown and black upperparts.
In winter, pale gray breast streaks on white underparts. Juveniles
are rusty above and streaked below. In flight, clear wing bar and
white rump divided by black.

Arctic breeder. On migration and in winter, seen at mud flats,
small pools and beaches. Mannerisms include a "stitching"
feeding action. Round-shouldered in appearance. Gregarious, it
disturbs in wheeling flocks with shrill notes.

(Summer) none. (Winter) **Red Knot:** straight bill, scaly gray back
markings. Small **"Peep" Sandpipers:** small size, slimmer build,
comparatively short bills, "scaly" backs. **Solitary** and **Stilt
Sandpipers:** long bills, long legs. **Pectoral Sandpiper:** longish
legs, "scaly" back.

Narrow-striped buff head and breast contrast sharply with white belly.

Plump profile. Striping strongest on breeding males. Female, juvenile, winter plumages all similar. Bill quite short, back dark brown with pale "scales." White rump divided by black stripe. Muddy-yellow legs.

Migrating from the Arctic to South America, these birds are found widely in wet meadows, marshes, pool and pond margins.

Other **Sandpipers** lack the abrupt contrast in markings but "**Peeps**" much smaller with black legs except for **Least** which is very small. **Solitary** has white rump divided and crossed by bars. **Stilt**: white rump not divided at all. **Red Knot** (winter): pale back, larger size.

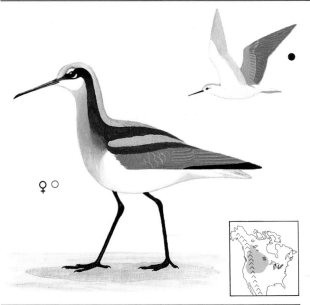

♀ ○

(**Summer only**) black eye stripe extends down neck becoming red-brown in color. Slender bill.

Long thin bill. White above and below eye stripe. Dark back with pale gray streaks, white underparts. In flight, dark wings contrast with white rump. Winter plumage is gray and white only, muddy-yellow legs.

Elegant birds with a curious habit of spinning on the water to disturb prey. This summer visitor to lakes, ponds, marshes across the continent, mainly in west and on Great Lakes, is commonly seen on migration to South America.

(Summer) none. (Winter) **Lesser Yellowlegs**: much larger and darker, with bright yellow legs.

RUDDY TURNSTONE
Internal Migrant

Distinctive black, white and ruddy brown wing pattern, with
black and white head. Colors fade in winter but the markings
remain recognizable.

Described as "harlequin" patterned with a "tortoiseshell" back
plumage, the other markings of this striking bird are a white belly
and breast, black bib, and very obvious orange legs. A stocky
shorebird with a short bill. Sexes alike.

Breeds on the Arctic tundra, and is seen as a passage migrant or
winter visitor. Jerky actions and short skittering runs are broken
by pauses to feed, turning over stones and shells. Seen on rocky
shorelines and on mud flats.

None.

KILLDEER

10½in

Resident/Summer Visitor

Two prominent black breast bands.

Black bands across front of crown and around eye. Brown upperparts with orange-brown rump. White underparts, wing bar and outer tail feathers. The tail is long and diamond-shaped.

Common in farm fields, parkland, lawns, airports and river banks. This species feeds on insects and worms and is familiar from coast to coast. The noisy call "kill-deeeah" gives rise to its name. Feigns injury when in danger.

Semipalmated Plover: single breast band, orange legs.

85

LESSER GOLDEN PLOVER
Internal Migrant   10½in

Bill-shape, golden brown back and lack of wing stripe.

Back is flecked with gold. In breeding plumage, face and
underparts are black except for white stripe from forehead, down
neck and sides of breast. In winter, plumage is speckled brown,
paler below. Juveniles similar.

This species breeds on the Arctic tundra. It may be seen inland on
migration in flocks on fields. It winters mainly along the
southwest coast, favoring mud flats and shorelines.

Black-bellied Plovers are a much paler silvery gray, and look
noticeably larger. They show a bold wing stripe. No other
Shorebirds share the bill size and overall proportions.

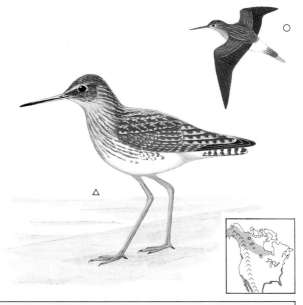

Medium sized wading bird with orange-yellow legs and medium
length straight bill.

Brown back flecked with black in breeding plumage and with
white in juvenile plumage (illustrated.) Pale underparts, heavily
streaked on the head, neck and upper breast, less so on the flanks.
White belly, rump and pale tail.

Nest on tundra, wintering mainly in South America. However
they are commonly seen in the east in marshes, on mud flats and
coastal locations. The call is fainter than the **Greater Yellowlegs**,
the "yew" being repeated once or twice only.

Greater Yellowlegs: larger with fairly long, slightly uptilted bill.
Willet: larger with black and white wings, bluish gray legs. Other
yellow-legged **Shorebirds** are notably smaller.

87

COMMON SNIPE
Internal Migrant

10½in

Rapid, zig-zag flight with "scaap" alarm note.

Long bill. Brown, black and white overall, with head and neck heavily striped and the flanks barred. The belly is white and the short legs are a muddy green. The back is noticeably striped with buff and the orange tail is edged with white.

Widespread and common, this species is noted for sitting tight, flushing late, with flight as above. During display dives, tail feathers vibrate giving a resonant drumming sound. Found in wet meadows, bogs, marshes.

Stilt Sandpiper (summer): long green legs, white rump. All other long-billed, stocky **Shorebirds** lack the heavy barring and striping, and do not fly in erratic zig-zags.

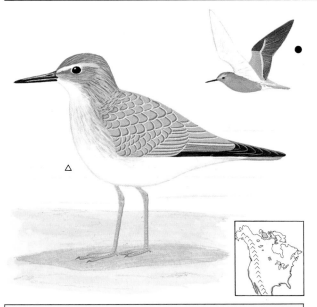

Extremely gregarious. Stout, short-legged shorebird with scaly gray markings on back. In summer has chestnut-red face and underparts.

Bill is straight and short. Pale wing bar visible in flight, as is pale rump and tail. Winter and juvenile's plumages are gray above with nearly white underparts and some streaking on the upper breast.

An Arctic breeder, this species is normally seen on migration, or wintering in large numbers feeding on mud flats and beaches. Often associates with other Shorebirds, notably Dowitchers. Call-note is "nut" and flight-call "twit-it."

Most **Shorebirds** are visibly slimmer in build but note **Dunlin** (winter): smaller bird, downcurved bill, white rump divided by black. **Dowitchers**: much longer bills, white wedge up the back.

BLACK-BELLIED PLOVER
Internal Migrant   **11in**

A bulky silvery gray shorebird with a white rump visible in flight.

In breeding plumage the face, breast and belly are black. The forehead, crown, nape, sides of breast form a white stripe. In winter the whole bird appears gray, paler below. Black wing-pits and a bold white wing stripe visible in flight.

Breeds on the Arctic tundra. Winters coastally around beaches, or marshy ground, mud flats. It is usually seen singly or in small numbers. A wary bird. Normally seen at a distance, its large size is distinctive.

Lesser Golden Plover: slightly smaller with browner "golden" coloring. No other **Shorebirds** share the bill size and overall proportions.

Long bill, a white wedge up the dark back, a "tu-tu-tu" alarm call.

All brown bird, heavily flecked, streaked and barred with black. Belly less marked. Prominent pale eyebrow. In breeding plumage the brown is reddish, turning gray-brown in winter. The juvenile is illustrated.

A bird of shallow water, especially open mud flats, this species is usually seen on migration. It feeds with a rapid "stitching" action. It is a shy bird, and will disturb easily, giving the identifying alarm call.

Long-billed Dowitcher: "keek" alarm call. **Marbled Godwit**: far larger, plain brown back. upturned bill. **Yellowlegs**: yellow-legged. **Pectoral**, **Stilt Sandpiper**: smaller, all brown back. **Red Knot**, **Common Snipe**: all brown back.

LONG-BILLED DOWITCHER
Winter Visitor/Internal Migrant   11½in

Long bill, a white wedge up the dark back, a "keek" alarm call.

All brown bird, heavily flecked, streaked and barred with black.
Belly less marked. Prominent pale eyebrow. In breeding plumage
the brown is reddish, turning to gray-brown in winter. The
juvenile is illustrated.

Highly migratory, this species winters from southern U.S. and
west coast down into South America. A bird of shallow water, it
feeds with a rapid "stitching" action. It is a shy bird, and will
disturb easily, giving the identifying alarm call.

Short-billed Dowitcher: "tu-tu-tu" alarm call. **Marbled Godwit**:
far larger, plain brown back, upturned bill. **Yellowlegs**: yellow-
legged. **Pectoral, Stilt Sandpiper**: smaller, all brown back. **Red
Knot, Common Snipe**: all brown back.

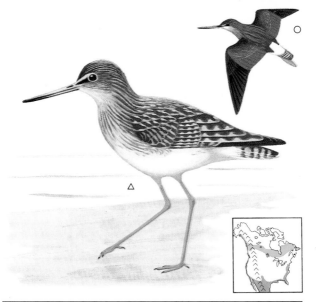

Large wading bird with orange-yellow legs and fairly long, slightly uptilted bill.

Brown back flecked with black in breeding plumage and with white in juvenile plumage (illustrated.) Pale underparts, heavily streaked on the head, neck, upper breast. Sides, belly less marked, especially in winter. White rump, pale tail.

Nests on tundra and winters widely across south and coasts, favoring marshes, mud flats and inland lakes and ponds. The call is usually a sequence of three "yew" notes.

Lesser Yellowlegs: smaller with medium length straight bill. **Willet**: black and white wings, bluish gray legs. Other yellow-legged **Shorebirds** are far smaller.

♂

Long red legs, out of proportion to size of the body.

Black wings, mantle, back of neck and head. Black needle-bill.
White elsewhere with a small white patch above the eye. The
juvenile has dark brown rather than black plumage.

Unique in its proportions, this elegant Shorebird flies with its long
legs trailing behind. It breeds locally in marshes, shallow lakes
and ponds, wintering mainly along the Mexican and Central
American coastline.

American Avocet: conspicuously upturned slender bill.

Large black and white-winged wading bird with a straight bill and bluish gray legs.

Nondescript gray-brown above, paler below. Summer breeding plumage shows streaking. Bill is straight, fairly heavy and medium length. Juveniles show a brown "scaly" back.

Rather local but numerous where found. Noisy and prominent, this species prefers marshes, shores and wet meadows. In the winter restricted to coastal regions. The name derives from its call, "pill-will-willet."

Greater and **Lesser Yellowlegs**, **Short** and **Long-billed Dowitchers**: smaller with plain dark wings. **American Avocet**: conspicuous slender upturned bill. Other **Shorebirds** with black and white wings are all small.

Long, downcurved bill and strongly striped crown.

The body is mainly gray-brown with the underparts paler than the back and the belly off-white. There is also an eye stripe in addition to those over the crown. Gray legs.

The species spends the summer breeding on the tundra, migrating to more southerly coasts where it may be seen in wet fields, marshes, mud flats and beaches. Typical call is a sequence of whistles.

Long-billed Curlew: very long, downcurved bill. **Glossy/White-faced Ibises**: glossy green and purple plumage. Other **Shorebirds** are nearly all smaller and have straighter and shorter bills.

AMERICAN AVOCET

Conspicuously upturned slender bill.

Upperparts are black and white. Underparts are white with long blue-gray legs. Head and long neck are orange-brown in summer, pale gray in winter. Sexes are alike, although the female's bill is more upturned.

Very distinctive, this elegant Shorebird feeds sweeping the bill from side to side, skimming food from the mud. A reasonably common species of shallow water locations, lakes, marshes, ponds. Call is a loud "wheek." Legs trail in flight.

Godwits have the tips of their long bills slightly upturned, but their build and coloring is very different. **Black-necked Stilt**: black and white plumage, but straight bill and extremely long reddish legs.

Large shorebird, with a long slightly upturned bill.

The whole body is buff brown, blended with dark brown above and barred below. The bill is orange-brown at the base, shading to a dark tip. The legs are gray.

This large bird uses its long legs and long bill to wade and feed in pools and lake margins to a greater depth than many other shorebirds. It nests mainly on the Great Plains, close to water, migrating to the coasts in winter.

Whimbrel, Long-billed Curlew: markedly downcurved bills. **Willet, Greater** and **Lesser Yellowlegs, Short** and **Long-billed Dowitchers**: much smaller with shorter straight bills. **Common Snipe**: much smaller.

Very long, downcurved bill. Cinnamon brown back.

The body is mainly cinnamon brown with the underparts notably darker and ruddier than the Whimbrel. The wing-pits are cinnamon. Gray legs.

A more inland species than the Whimbrel, these curlew breed on dry uplands as well as wet locations. In winter seen in a wide variety of habitats from farmland to freshwater, saltwater margins, marshes and mud flats. The call is an eerie "cur-lee."

Whimbrel: shorter downcurved bill, strongly striped crown.
Glossy/White-faced Ibises: glossy green and purple plumage.
Other **Shorebirds** are nearly all smaller and have shorter and straighter bills.

Smallest tern, with a forked tail, white forehead. Breeding adults have a yellow bill.

Yellow bill has black tip. Black capped, pale gray above, white below. Juveniles, immatures and winter adults have blackish or black bills, and show a dark shoulder bar. Breeding adults have black outer primaries.

Nests colonially on coastal beaches and on sandbars and estuaries inland. As it is so small flight is very buoyant and the wingbeats very fast. Extremely aggressive for its size.

Other **Terns** are much larger, except for **Black Tern**: non-breeding birds have dark wings. Small **Gulls** are larger and lack forked tail.

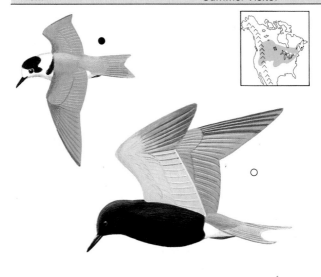

Dark wings, notched tail. Breeding adults have black bodies.

Wings and cleft tail are all gray, the undertail coverts are white, the bill is black and the short legs are blood-red. First summer immatures are distinctively blotched black on the body, as are molting adults later in the summer.

A summer visitor from South America, this species is typical of terns, a buoyant bounding flier with pointed wings, checking to plunge-dive for prey. It feeds at lakes and marshes, sometimes far inland. It usually migrates coastally.

Other **Terns** are much larger, except for **Least Tern** which has paler wings and a more forked tail in all plumages. Small **Gulls** are larger and lack forked tail.

101

A small black-billed gull. Adults have a black hood and white
wedge at wing tips.

Adults: back and most of wings gray, a white body, red legs. In
fall, hood is replaced by a dark ear spot. Immatures lack full hood,
show brown bar on inner wing, some of white wedge, black tail
band. Adult plumage in second year.

Buoyant in flight like terns, these active noisy gulls breed across
Canada on the lakes. They then migrate to more southerly
coastlines and especially the Great Lakes. Call of "churr" and
chattering notes.

Franklin's Gull: significantly hooded at all times, adults show a
distinct white band separating the gray wing from the black and
white wing tip. (Other hooded **Gulls** are coastal species and do not
share primary features above.) **Terns** are capped, never hooded,
with cleft or forked tails.

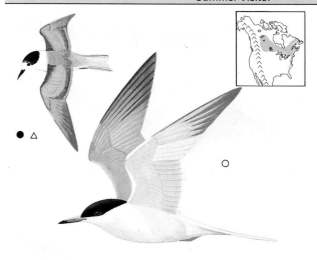

Adult: deeply forked tail. Red bill and feet. Primaries show wedge of dark gray. Juvenile/Immature: black all around nape.

Black capped. Red bill has black tip. Medium gray above and very pale gray below. Juveniles, immatures, and winter adults show pinkish or black bills, and also a dark shoulder bar which is lacking on Forster's Tern.

Exclusively associated with water they feed by plunge-diving for fish. Flight is buoyant and bounding. A summer visitor, this is a common species and can be found breeding in huge colonies, widely across Canada and northern U.S.

Forster's Tern: orange bill and feet, primaries very pale gray. Non-breeding bird's eye patch does not go around nape. Other **Terns** have yellow, black, or heavy red bills. **Gulls** lack the deeply forked tail, have heavier build.

Significantly hooded in all ages and seasons, adults have a distinctive white band separating the gray wing from the black and white wing tip. The bill is delicate.

Small, red-billed gull, slate gray above, white body, breast pinkish at close range. In fall, nape remains dark. First summer immatures not fully hooded, have black bills, lack distinctive white band. Adult plumage in second year.

Unlike most gulls, this visitor breeds well inland in marsh and lake locations. However, it winters at sea off the South American Pacific Coast, and is seen on migration along the western seaboard. Crying call with "kuk-kuk" notes.

Bonaparte's Gull: only breeding adults are hooded, white wedge at wing tips. (Other hooded **Gulls** are coastal species and do not share primary features above.) **Terns** are capped, never hooded, with cleft or forked tails.

104

Adult has deeply forked tail, orange bill and feet, primaries show wedge of very pale gray. Juvenile/immature/winter: black eye patch does not go around the nape.

Black capped. Orange bill has black tip. Pale gray above and very white below. Juveniles, immatures and winter adults show pinkish or black bills, and lack the shoulder bar which is seen on Common Terns.

Widespread, including a resident area on the Gulf Coast, Forster's Terns nest colonially in marshy habitats. As with other terns, they plunge-dive for fish, from a buoyant and bounding flight.

Common Tern: red bill and feet. Outer primaries dark gray. Non-breeding birds have black all way around nape. Other **Terns** have yellow, black, or heavy red bills. **Gulls** lack the deeply forked tail, have heavier build.

105

Adults have yellow legs. The yellow bill is entirely encircled by a black ring.

Gray back and wings, black-tipped with white spots. Head, tail, underparts white, with head brown-speckled in winter. Immatures show varying brown plumage, dark bills, for two years. The light build identifies with practice.

An abundant species. Although common in coastal regions, it is also found inland around water, plowed fields and dumps, with the winter range more southerly than the central breeding habitat.

Adults: other **Gulls** lack bill ring and yellow legs. Immatures: **California** and **Herring Gulls**: larger and stockier. (Other similar **Gulls** are coastal species only and do not share primary features above.) **Terns**: slimmer build, cleft or forked tails.

Adults have yellow-green legs and a yellow bill with both a red spot and a small black spot.

Adult has gray back and wings, tipped black and white, white tail, underparts and head. The head has brown speckles in winter. Juveniles and immatures show varying brown plumages for three years.

Common in the west, this species breeds inland, migrating to the west coast in winter. Although associated with water, it is very often seen some distance from any major wet habitat.

Adults: **Ring-billed Gull**: adults have yellow legs, the yellow bill is entirely encircled by a black ring. **Herring, Glaucous Gulls**: pink legs. (Other yellow-legged **Gulls** have no bill spot, or have dark gray backs with a red bill spot only.) **Terns**: slimmer build, cleft or forked tails.

Large size, forked tail and heavy red bill.

Heavy build, differing from gulls, with pointed wings typical of the tern. Adult's bill is black-tipped. Black capped, upperparts gray, underparts nearly white, a dark panel shows under the wing tips. Legs black. Non-breeding plumages similar.

Widespread, but only common locally, it breeds across the continent in suitable marsh, inland lake and coastal habitats. A large bird, the flight is less bounding than smaller relatives. It plunge-dives from a greater height.

Other **Terns** are much smaller, with **Common** and **Forster's** having deeply forked tails. **Gulls** lack the forked tail and have more rounded wings.

Adults have pale gray back, black-tipped wings, pink legs.

Adults: gray wings, white head, tail and underparts. A heavy yellow bill with red spot. In winter, neck and breast become speckled brown. Immatures show varying brown plumages and dark bills for three years. Very uniformly dark.

Although common in coastal regions, this abundant species is found inland as well. A raucous scavenger, frequently found at dumps.

Adult: **California, Ring-billed Gulls**: smaller, yellow legs. **Glaucous Gull**: larger, either pale gray or white back and wings with white primaries. (Other similar **Gulls** are coastal species only, with either dark gray backs or no black wing tips.) **Terns**: slimmer, cleft or forked tails.

109

Very large gull with either pale gray or white back and wings, and white-tipped primaries.

A heavily built gull with a white body and pink legs. The head becomes flecked with brown in winter. The bill is yellow with a red spot. Juveniles and immatures show some brown giving a "dirty" appearance.

Breeds in the high Arctic tundra. Partially resident in Alaska, normally seen on the Great Lakes and northern coasts in winter. Impressive, the largest pale gull, it prefers carrion to taking prey. Solitary by nature.

Herring Gull: smaller and darker backed with black wing tips. Other **Gulls** are either similar in size but darker backed, or are smaller. **Terns**: far smaller with cleft or forked tails.

White bodied bird of prey that plunges into water trapping fish in its talons.

Upperparts are dark brown with a brown band through eye. The remainder of head and upperparts are predominantly white. The underside of the wings show a dark "wrist," and "fingers." The wing span is 5–6 feet.

Ospreys fly with arched wings, their long narrow shape enabling them to hover over prey before plunging. Not common but widespread, seen on bare perches and large stick nests near water. They eat only fish.

Bald Eagle: far larger. Head is all white in adults, and all ages have brown bodies. **Swallow-tailed Kite**: much smaller body, long forked tail.

Huge size and white head in adults. Immatures have white areas in inner underwing.

The adult is dark brown backed with a very white tail and a heavy hooked yellow bill. Immatures are all dark, including the bill, for several years. The above-mentioned white areas are gradually replaced by the adult's dark plumage.

America's national bird, it is now regaining its numbers. Normally associated with rivers, lakes and coasts, it feeds mainly on fish.

Osprey: white body, plunges for fish. Much smaller. (Eagles and Vultures which might appear similar in high flight do not frequent wet habitats and certainly lack the adult's white head.)

Entirely dark gray. Plump shape.

Short bill, black in adults. Juvenile birds have pale bills, and paler underparts. Tail and wings are short, giving a rapid, direct flight. Note the white eyelid membrane for underwater protection.

Always associated with fast-running water, these little birds patrol a fixed territory. When at rest they curtsy and bob repeatedly. They can swim, dive and, quite remarkably, "walk" along a stream bottom while searching for prey.

None.

BELTED KINGFISHER

Internal Migrant

♂

♀

A typical kingfisher plunging for fish, with blue-gray back and white belly.

Blue-gray crested head, breast bar, wings and tail. The female additionally has a rust colored belly and flank bar. Note the dagger-like bill.

This is the only common American kingfisher and is found along streams, lakes, estuaries and coasts. It nests in holes in banks. Often seen apparently out of habitat on telegraph wires.

None.

All black with short "ca" call-note.

Marginally the smallest crow, juveniles are less well feathered than their parents.

A water-associated species found close to river valleys, marshes in eastern U.S. Largely resident, some migration takes place mainly along rivers. Omnivorous, diet is grain, insects, reptiles, dead fish, other carrion, fruit.

American Crow: call is "caw" or "carr."

Open wetlands, grassland & fields

Short-eared Owl (1)
15in   Internal Migrant
Open country owl with black
around eyes and black "wrist"
patches.

Northern Harrier (2)
17–24in   Internal Migrant
White rump. Long slim wings
for low-level low speed flight.

Swallow-tailed Kite (3)
24in   Summer Visitor
Black and white with deeply
forked tail.

Sandhill Crane (4)
42in   Internal Migrant
Untidy "bustle" at rear
overhangs tail feathers.

Common Yellowthroat (1)
5in Resident/Summer Visitor
Plain olive above (no wing bars) contrasting with very yellow throat. Male also has heavy black mask.

Red-winged Blackbird (2)
8½in Resident/Summer Visitor
Sharp pointed bill. Male: red-shouldered black bird. Female: very heavily streaked underparts.

Yellow-headed Blackbird (3)
9½in Resident/Summer Visitor
Sharp pointed bill. Orange-yellow throat and breast. Male: black back, yellow head. Female: brown back.

Common Grackle (4)
12½in Resident/Summer Visitor
Remarkable keel-shaped tail.

Bogs, swamps, wooded bogs, ponds

Swamp Sparrow (1)
5½in Internal Migrant
Summer adults have rust colored
cap, gray eyebrow stripe and
white throat. In winter central
cap shows gray.

Empidonax Flycatchers:
Yellow-bellied (2), Alder (3)
5¼–5¾in Summer Visitors
Flycatching behavior. Both have
2 wing bars and a pale eye ring.

Vermillion Flycatcher (4)
6in Internal Migrant
Male: brilliant red cap and
underparts. Female: soft pink
tinge on belly, overlaid with
streaks.

Northern Waterthrush (5)
6in Summer Visitor
Uniformly cream, heavily
streaked underparts. Cream or
buff eyebrow stripe. Slim build.

Yellow Warbler (1)
5in Summer Visitor
Almost entirely yellow or yellow-green. Even tail spots are yellow.

Tree Swallow (2)
5¾in Internal Migrant
Swallow-type, all white below, entirely blue-green above (brown above in immatures.)

Eastern Kingbird (3)
8½in Summer Visitor
Flycatching behavior. White band at tip of tail.

Red-shouldered Hawk (4)
20in Resident/Summer Visitor
Broad tail bands. Adult: red shoulders and reddish body.

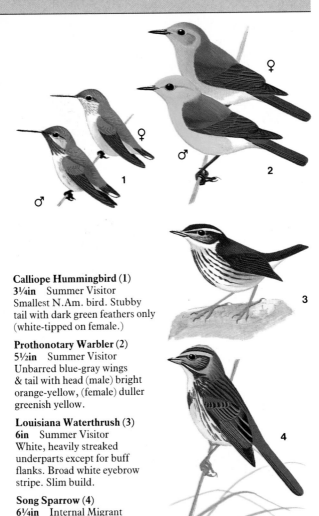

Calliope Hummingbird (1)
3¼in Summer Visitor
Smallest N.Am. bird. Stubby
tail with dark green feathers only
(white-tipped on female.)

Prothonotary Warbler (2)
5½in Summer Visitor
Unbarred blue-gray wings
& tail with head (male) bright
orange-yellow, (female) duller
greenish yellow.

Louisiana Waterthrush (3)
6in Summer Visitor
White, heavily streaked
underparts except for buff
flanks. Broad white eyebrow
stripe. Slim build.

Song Sparrow (4)
6¼in Internal Migrant
Whitish, streaked breast. Long
rounded tail. Both crown and
eyebrow stripes vary in color.

Vaux's Swift (1)
4½in   Summer Visitor
Tiny, long-winged swallow-type
with stubby tail. West of
Rockies only.

Bank Swallow (2)
5¼in   Summer Visitor
Swallow-type, brown above with
brown breastband across white
underparts.

**Northern Rough-winged
Swallow (3)**
5½in   Summer Visitor
Swallow-type, brown above with
chin to breast a gray-brown
tinge.

American Crow (4)
18½in   Resident/Summer
Visitor
Entirely black with "caw" and
"carr" call-notes.

121

Index and check-list

Keep a record of your sightings by checking the box.